Incredible Molluscs

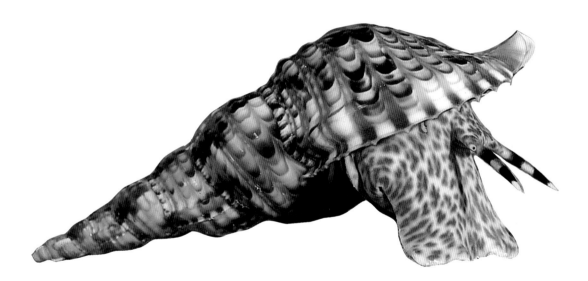

John Townsend

www.raintreepublishers.co.uk
Visit our website to find out more information about **Raintree** books.

To order:
☎ Phone 44 (0) 1865 888113
🖷 Send a fax to 44 (0) 1865 314091
🖳 Visit the Raintree Bookshop at **www.raintreepublishers.co.uk** to browse our catalogue and order online.

First published in Great Britain by Raintree, Halley Court, Jordan Hill, Oxford OX2 8EJ, part of Harcourt Education. Raintree is a registered trademark of Harcourt Education Ltd.

Editorial: Charlotte Guillain and Diyan Leake
Design: Michelle Lisseter and Kamae Design
Picture Research: Maria Joannou
Production: Jonathan Smith

Originated by Ambassador Litho Ltd
Printed and bound in Hong Kong, China by South China Printing Company

ISBN 1 844 43326 9
08 07 06 05 04
10 9 8 7 6 5 4 3 2 1

British Library Cataloguing in Publication Data
Townsend, John
Incredible Molluscs. – (Incredible Creatures)
594
A full catalogue record for this book is available from the British Library.

Acknowledgements
The publisher would like to thank the following for permission to reproduce photographs: Alamy Images p. 12 left (IMAGINA/Atsushi Tsunoda); Christine Osborne World Religions p. 38 left; Corbis pp. 4 (Todd A. Gipstein), 14 left (Stuart Westmorland), 36 right (Stuart Westmorland), 47 right (Peter Steiner), 48 (Paul A. Souders), 49 left (Araldo de Luca); FLPA pp. 5 left (F. Bavendam), 6 left (Roger Wilmshurst), 8–9 (D. P. Wilson), 10–11 (F. Bavendam), 11 right (F. Lanting), 12–13 (A. Wharton), 14–15 (Michael Rose), 16 left (Michael Rose), 18 inset (D. P. Wilson), 18 main (Peter David), 23 left (Gerard Lacz), 23 right (Tony Hamblin), 26 bottom (F. Bavendam), 30–1 (Derek Middleton), 31 right (Colin Marshall), 32–3 (B. Cranston), 46 left (Martin Witherg); Hawaii Photo Resource pp. 20–1 (Jack Jeffrey); Imagequest 3-D p. 28 left (James D. Watt); Mary Evans Picture Library p. 41 right; Nature Photographers p. 49 right; Nature Picture Library pp. 10 left (B. Jones & M. Shimlock), 22 (Jason Smalley), 25 right (Dietmar Nill), 29 right (Constantinos Petrinos), 28–9 (Jeff Rotman), 38–9 (Jeff Rotman); NHPA pp. 5 top (Lawrence Lawry), 5 middle (Karl Switak), 5 bottom (G. I. Bernard), 6–7 (Laurie Campbell), 7 right (Roy Waller), 9 right (E.A. Janes), 13 right (Pete Atkinson), 15 right (Matt Bain), 16–17 (Laurie Campbell), 17 right, 20 left (Daniel Heuclin), 26 top (Image Quest 3-D), 27 (Norbert Wu), 33 right (Norbert Wu), 34 left (B. Jones & M. Shimlock), 35 right (James Carmichael Jr), 40 top (ANT Photo Library), 40–1 (Norbert Wu), 42 (Lawrence Lawry), 43 top (ANT Photo Library), 44 top (Image Quest 3-D), 44–5 (Karl Switak), 46–7 (G. I. Bernard); Oxford Scientific Films pp. 8 left (John McCammon), 30 left, 32 left (Karen Gowlett-Holmes), 39 right (Howard Hall); Science Photo Library pp. 19 (Mauro Fermariello), 21 right (Clouds Hill Imaging Ltd), 24 (Peter Scoones), 25 left (Sinclair Stammers), 34–5 (Matthew Oldfield), 36 left (Jon Wilson), 37 (Georgette Duowma), 43 bottom, 50 (Ron Church), 51 (Tim Beddow); USDA p. 45 right (Aphis)

Cover photograph of a Roman snail reproduced with permission of Premaphotos Wildlife (Ken Preston-Mafham)

The publishers would like to thank Jon Pearce for his assistance in the preparation of this book.

Every effort has been made to contact copyright holders of any material reproduced in this book. Any omissions will be rectified in subsequent printings if notice is given to the publishers.

Contents

Any words appearing in the text in bold, **like this**, are explained in the Glossary. You can also look out for them in the Word bank at the bottom of each page.

The world of molluscs

Would you believe it?

- The largest sea snail, found off the coast of Australia, was a trumpet conch nearly 80 centimetres long. It weighed 18 kilograms.

- The largest land snail is the giant African snail. It can reach over 30 centimetres from head to tail. The largest can weigh 900 grams and its shell is bigger than a grapefruit.

- In the past, South Pacific islanders used mollusc shells as money.

They are slow, they are quiet and they are often out of sight. Yet molluscs are everywhere in huge numbers. After insects, molluscs have more **species** than any other group of animals on Earth. Some scientists think there could be over 100,000 different species. Others think there could be many more still to be discovered.

Molluscs live in a whole range of **habitats**. Most live in the sea, sometimes very deep. Others live in streams or on land, including deserts and mountains. Some scientists think molluscs were among the earliest forms of life on Earth, over 500 million years ago. For thousands of years they have been important to humans for food, money and jewellery. The silent world of molluscs still has many surprises.

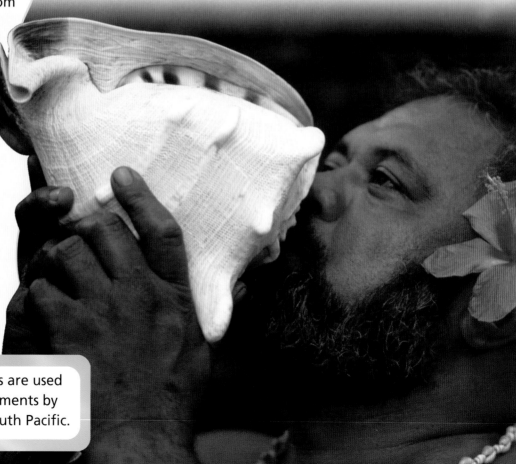

▶ Trumpet conches are used as musical instruments by people in the South Pacific.

habitat   natural home of an animal or plant
invertebrate   animal without a backbone

▲ Octopuses belong to the mollusc group called cephalopods.

Find out later...

What is special about an oyster's pearl?

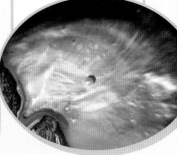

What are the problems with the biggest snail on Earth?

What is so important about mollusc slime?

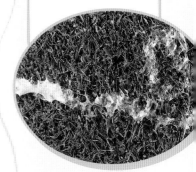

What is a mollusc?

Molluscs come in all sizes and shapes. The word 'mollusc' comes from the Latin word *mollis*. It simply means 'soft'. All molluscs have soft bodies and many have hard shells to protect these soft bodies. They are all **invertebrates,** which means they do not have backbones. Many move about on a flat pad called a foot. Sometimes their heads have bendy **tentacles** for holding food or for feeling.

The three main groups of molluscs are:

- **Gastropods**, which move along on their soft belly. There may be 70,000 different species, including snails, slugs and limpets.
- **Bivalves**, with two shells joined at a **hinge**. There may be 20,000 different species, including mussels, clams and oysters.
- **Cephalopods**, with tentacles coming from their head. There may be 650 different species, including squid, octopus and cuttlefish.

Other groups include sea worms, **chitons** and tusk shells.

tentacle   animal body part that is like a long, thin arm

Meet the family

Each mollusc group has some amazing family members.

Long and short

The great grey slug (below) is sometimes 10 centimetres long. It is a European species but it has been carried around the world on plants and fruit. It is now common in eastern North America. The **native** American slug is much smaller, often less than 2.5 centimetres long.

Quite often the bigger species eats all the food. The smallest species then has nothing to eat.

Gastropods

Gastropods are animals that move along on their soft bellies. The belly is like a foot that slowly pushes them along. The best known gastropods are slugs and snails.

Many snails have two **tentacles**, like horns, that wave about on top of their heads. These tentacles have eyes on the end. Snails can be as small as 0.1 centimetre long, but they are usually a few centimetres long. Land snails like damp places but they can **adapt** to changes in moisture. Some desert snails can stay sealed in their thick shells for over a year if there is no rain.

There are also many **species** of sea slugs and snails. These often have bright colours and patterns.

muscular   has strong muscles
native   belonging to that particular place

Limpets and periwinkles

'To cling like a limpet' means to hold on really tightly. Limpets are molluscs that grip on to rocks so hard that even the most determined **predator** cannot get them off. Limpets are left clinging to rocks when the tide goes out. They have a **muscular** foot that clamps down tightly on to the rock so nothing can prise them off. Rocks are often covered with these clinging shells at low tide. When the tide comes in again, they let go and move over the rocks looking for food. They feed on seaweed.

Periwinkles are sea snails that live on seashores around the world. When a periwinkle hides in its shell, it closes a hard plate behind it to stop anything getting in to eat it.

Whelks

Whelks are larger than periwinkles, with spiral shells up to 24 centimetres long. They eat other molluscs using a long sharp tongue, as seen below. They poke this into the shells of oysters and mussels. Then they spit an acid that breaks down the animal's body, which they slurp up like a milkshake!

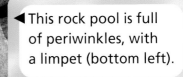
◄ This rock pool is full of periwinkles, with a limpet (bottom left).

predator   animal that hunts and eats other animals
whelk   gastropod that lives in the sea and has a spiral shell

Molluscs that wreck boats

Boring clams got their name because they bore holes through wood. Shipworms like the one below are actually clams rather than worms. They can do a lot of damage to wooden boats, boring through a thick plank of wood in less than one year.

Bivalves

Bivalves are molluscs with two shells joined by a **hinge**. The two halves are called valves and they open and close. People eat bivalves as seafood and call them shellfish, although they are not fish.

Oysters and clams

Oysters often live in groups called oyster beds. Beds of bluepoint oysters are found along the eastern coast of North America. Chesapeake Bay, in the USA, is the largest oyster-producing area in the world. Oysters are unable to move on their own but they are carried by waves.

Clams are bivalves with thick, heavy, heart-shaped shells.

FAST FACTS

The quahog is an ocean clam named by Native Americans. It can live to be 220 years old.

gland   part of the body that makes hormones and other substances
propel   drive or push forward

Mussels, scallops and cockles

Bivalves often have a fleshy covering along the edge of the shells. Some have waving **tentacles** with tiny eyes on the ends.

There are many different types of mussel and they are all related to **scallops, cockles** and oysters. The blue mussel has a blue-black shell up to 11 centimetres long. When the mussel is closed, its large **muscular** foot is usually the only body part that can be seen. At the end of this foot, there is a **gland** that makes a thread. The mussel uses this thread to move or to cling on to rocks.

There are hundreds of **species** of scallops and cockles, which are similar to clams and oysters. They feed on tiny sea plants and animals.

◀ Mussels hold on to rocks using thin, sticky threads.

Useful shells

- Shells keep molluscs safe. Yet birds such as the oystercatcher above have hard beaks like chisels that can lever open mussel and oyster shells. They can get inside quickly to scoop out the mollusc.

- Scallops and some other bivalves move by pushing out water. By quickly shutting their shells, they squeeze out water. This **propels** them along like a jet.

scallop   a bivalve mollusc with semicircular shells with wavy edges

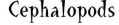

Cephalopods

Cephalopods are different from other molluscs. They still have soft bodies with **tentacles** but some can move really fast. They often have very long tentacles around their heads.

There are about 650 species of octopus, squid and cuttlefish. Both octopuses and squid have a mouth like a parrot's beak but they have no outside shell. Many species live in the deepest parts of the ocean. An octopus has eight tentacles of the same length and a funnel through which water can be squirted to **propel** it along.

The squid has ten tentacles, and two of them are much longer than the others. These are usually pulled back into two pockets near its mouth. The giant squid can weigh up to 2000 kilograms and is the largest **invertebrate** on Earth.

Many arms

The word 'cephalopod' means 'head-footed'. These molluscs have feet that seem to come out of their heads. All octopuses have eight tentacles, while squid and cuttlefish (shown above) have ten. The nautilus can have 30 to 90 tentacles.

► The Maori octopus lives in the sea off Australia.

calcium   mineral that animals need in food for strong bones and teeth

Cuttlefish

Cuttlefish look like small, flattened squid with a fin running round their bodies. They have a shell-like bone inside their bodies. The shells of dead cuttlefish (cuttlebones) are often washed up on beaches. These cuttlebones are given to birds, as they are full of **calcium** and are good for parrots to peck.

Some species of cuttlefish swim in groups and they are found in many tropical waters. The giant cuttlefish is found in the waters off southern Australia. It can reach 1 metre long and weigh 3 kilograms.

Only one type of cephalopod has a spiral shell like other molluscs. This is the nautilus. It swims along the sea-bed using its tentacles to find **prey**. A nautilus can dive to depths of 500 metres and travel up to 1 kilometre (0.6 miles) in one day.

A tough life

Eels, sharks, swordfish, penguins, seals, whales, dolphins and humans are just some of the **predators** that find cephalopods tasty. If they are lucky, octopuses can live for about three years. Larger cephalopods and those in very cold waters may live longer. The giant squid and the giant octopus are thought to live for up to five years.

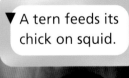
▼ A tern feeds its chick on squid.

tentacle   animal body part that is like a long, thin arm

Shapes of mollusc shells

- A **gastropod** shell can be shaped like a cap, an ear, a pear, a corkscrew, an egg or a mixture of all of these.

- A **bivalve** can look like a frisbee, a fan, a triangle, a long boat or it can be heart-shaped.

- A tusk shell is shaped like a curved elephant's tusk.

- A chiton is shaped like a shield.

Odds and ends

There are many **species** of mollusc that do not fit into the three main groups. These all have their own special differences.

Chitons are sometimes called 'coat of mail' shells as they have eight overlapping shell-plates that look like a suit of armour. They have no eyes. There are about 550 different species of this mollusc. The largest can be over 40 centimetres long. Chitons live in the sea and in rock pools. They press their bodies hard to the ground like limpets and cannot be prised off. They are more active at night, because during the day they tend to cling to the underside of rocks and ledges. Chitons are **herbivores** and feed on **algae** growing on rocks.

> To find out more about how molluscs breathe, look at pages 16 and 17.

▲ Here a chiton sticks to a rock with a limpet as a neighbour.

Wild words   algae   types of simple plant without stems that grow in water or on rocks

Tusk shells

There are about 350 different species of tusk shell that live in the sea. They bury into sand and stick up like an elephant's tusk. They range in size from just 2 millimetres long to 15 centimetres. They all feed by spreading their tiny **tentacles** down into the sand.

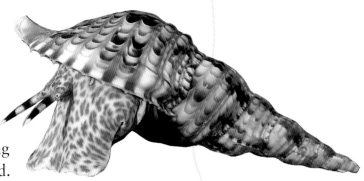

Other molluscs

There are about 250 species of worm-like mollusc, sometimes living at very great depths in the oceans. They have no shell and can grow to 30 centimetres long.

▲ This Triton trumpet shell is one of the biggest sea snails.

Length of largest molluscs (in metres)

giant squid	16.77
giant clam	1.40
Australian trumpet	0.80
Hexabranchus	0.52
Steller's coat	0.47
freshwater mussel	0.30

herbivore   animal that only eats plants – a vegetarian

Amazing bodies

Walkabout

Some **species** of octopus can leave the water to hunt for food such as shrimps and other molluscs in rock pools. The Caribbean reef octopus, like the one below from the Florida Keys, USA, has been seen crawling over rocks and even up walls. It can only stay out of water for a few minutes at a time as it cannot breathe without lungs.

Cephalopods can move in three ways. They can push a jet of water out through a funnel to **propel** them along, they can flap their **tentacles** like wings and they can walk along the ocean floor. The funnel can turn in any direction, which means they can move in any direction. If you want to catch an octopus, your chances are better at night. That is because they move up to the surface of the sea at night and go back down at dawn.

Cuttlefish glide through the water by gently rippling their skirt-like fins. They can go up or down by changing the amount of liquid or air inside their bones.

Squid can swim faster than any other **invertebrate** by letting water into their bodies and squirting it out at high speed.

cockle   sea mollusc that has a ribbed bivalve shell

Getting about

Some **bivalves**, such as **cockles**, move along the sea-bed by jumping. Their feet act like springs that keep kicking them forward. Oysters cannot move like this as they have a much smaller foot. They rely on waves and **currents** to carry them.

Scallops swim in jerky movements through the water by slamming shut their two shells. The constant opening and shutting forces out water. This propels them along.

Mussels live glued to rocks, bigger shells or other mussels. They also cling to piers or sea walls. A **gland** in the mussel's foot makes a fine line of glue that hardens in the water and becomes a strong thread. The mussel holds on and can pull itself along this thread – and even use it to tie up **predators** such as snails.

Moving at the speed of a snail

The common garden snail takes more than three minutes just to move 1 metre. At this rate, it would take over two days to travel 1 kilometre (0.6 miles). It is just as well they are never in a hurry!

◄ This cockle orb shell is a bivalve mollusc.

current   body of water that moves in a particular direction

Keeping alive

All land slugs and snails breathe air using lungs while all water molluscs take oxygen from the water through gills. Water has to keep passing through the mollusc so that its gills can get oxygen from the water. It then absorbs oxygen into its blood vessels.

Breathing

All animals need **oxygen** to live. They must breathe by taking in oxygen from the surrounding air or water. Blood carries this oxygen to the brain and muscles. Land animals breathe using lungs, while fish and other sea animals breathe with **gills**. The gills are slits which take oxygen from water flowing through them.

So if molluscs get oxygen from water, how do they cope when the tide goes out and they are left high and dry? They must keep wet. Limpets trap a tiny puddle of water in their shell. Keyhole limpets fan this water over their gills and out of the 'keyhole' at the top of their shell. Other limpets have gills on the edge of their shells.

▲ The gills of this mussel take food as well as oxygen out of the water.

cilia   tiny hairs that wave together to make currents of movement
oxygen   one of the gases in air and water that all living things need

Gills

Most **bivalve** molluscs have one pair of long gills. Tiny hairs called **cilia** sweep water over the gills. Bivalves also use their gills to feed, by trapping food particles as well as oxygen.

Some mussels live in sea water and others live in fresh water. They all breathe with gills, and some **species** have two openings. Water flows in through one opening and out through the other. This is like breathing in through one nostril and breathing out through the other. They can spend time out of water and do not have to keep water flowing through them all the time like fish do.

Surviving

Most water molluscs, like the periwinkles below, can slow down their breathing out of water or when the tide is out. They can manage without oxygen until the tide comes back in. Some species even cope with freezing. Some types of periwinkle can **survive** to −20 °C, with 75 per cent of their body water being frozen.

▲ Mussels may be left high and dry at low tide.

Eyes everywhere

Some members of the scallop family, like the one below, have many eyes. They all help the scallop to see if a **predator** is coming. The eyes look in all directions and give warning signals when danger approaches. This gives the scallop enough time to clam up.

Sight

Although most molluscs have poor vision, **cephalopods** such as squid and octopuses can see well. Cephalopods have the most developed eyes of any **invertebrate**. The eyes of octopuses are as **complex** as those of mammals and are similar in many ways to human eyes. They can also turn like ours to look in any direction.

One type of squid has two eyes that are quite different from each other. One eye is twice as big as the other and looks like a tube with a yellow **lens**. It seems that the smaller eye is used to look at things close up and on the sea-bed. The larger eye seems to be used to view the world above. It may also be used to spot the faint lights given off by sea animals in their deep, dark world.

▲ For the size of its head, a squid's eyes are enormous.

　　complex　detailed and complicated

The giant squid is famous for its huge eyes. It has the largest eyes in the animal kingdom. They are **adapted** to see at great depths where there is little light.

Touch and smell

An octopus has a well-developed sense of touch. The rim of each sucker on its **tentacles** can feel many details. Studies have shown that a blindfolded octopus can tell the difference between objects of various shapes and sizes.

Some **gastropods** have a well-developed sense of smell. They can detect food in the water from a long distance.

▼ This octopus is doing a learning test in a laboratory tank.

Top of the class

Invertebrates are not known for being clever. Octopuses have the most complex brains of all the invertebrates. They even seem to remember things. They can learn to solve puzzles quite quickly. Although they cannot match many birds and mammals for brain power, they do very well for animals that do not live very long.

lens   clear, curved part of the eye

Feeding

Old shells

Molluscs grow their shells by absorbing **calcium** from the food they eat. Tiny shells, bones and fish contain a lot of calcium. By measuring how much calcium and other minerals are in mollusc shells, scientists can work out the quality of the water and their **habitat**.

Molluscs are like most other animals in that a lot of their time is spent trying to keep safe, looking for a mate or searching for food. Eating and finding the next meal can be a life's work.

Finding food

The wolf snail lives on land and tracks down its **prey** by going on the prowl like a wolf! Its favourite food is smaller snails. It finds them by following their trail of slime. Then it chases them. At least, it goes after them two to three times faster than a normal snail. When it catches up with its prey, the wolf snail eats tiny snails whole. It turns over larger snails and gets into their shells before eating them alive.

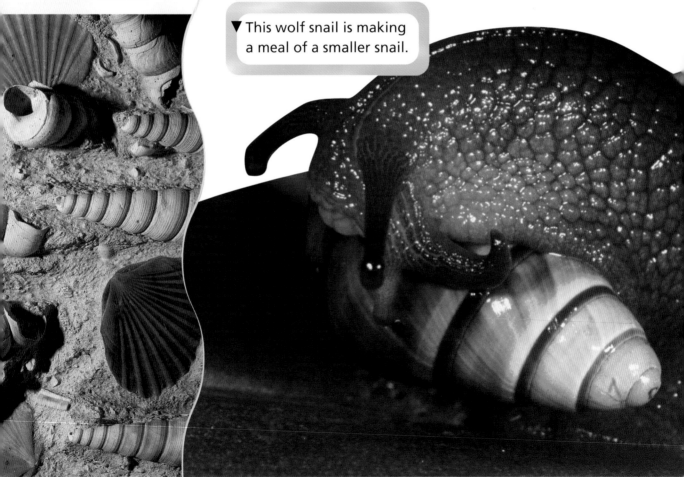

▼ This wolf snail is making a meal of a smaller snail.

acid   a liquid that can be stong enough to break down materials

Clever tricks

An octopus finds food such as crabs and other molluscs by using bait. It often attracts its victim by wiggling the tip of a **tentacle** to look like a worm in the sand. Then it sinks its sharp beak into the victim's shell and injects a poison that kills its prey.

The right tool for the job

Many molluscs have a special tongue called a **radula**, which is like a long rough file covered with tiny teeth. It is just right for poking into other shells or for getting weed out of rock cracks. It is pulled into and out of the mouth with a rasping motion. Only molluscs have this tool.

The number of teeth on the radula in different mollusc species varies from a few to many thousands. **Bivalves** are the only molluscs that do not have a radula.

Breaking into shells

Some sea snails are **predators** and use their radula (shown above) to bore holes through the shells of other molluscs. They then suck out the flesh. Some even make an **acid** that can eat through a mollusc's shell.

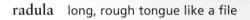
radula   long, rough tongue like a file

Ways of feeding

A large number of molluscs are **herbivores** or grazers, especially the **chitons** and many slugs and snails. Tusk shells feed on tiny bits of material that sink to the sea-bed. Most **bivalves** filter material and **sediment** from the water.

Herbivores

On land, molluscs are big plant-eaters. Any gardener's biggest enemies are bound to be slugs and snails. They are major pests in farming as they destroy young plants. Slugs also feed on many fruits and vegetables just before harvest. This feeding may not harm the fruit, but **bacteria** can get into the wounds and spoil the crop. Also, food covered in slime does not look very tasty.

Slugs hide in the day and eat plants at night. They eat small shoots and the edges of bigger leaves. Slugs often climb trees in search of food. To get down again they drop slowly on a slimy thread. Many birds, badgers and hedgehogs are natural **predators** of garden slugs.

▼ The slug is Plant Enemy Number 1.

anus   opening at the very end of the digestive passage
bacteria   group of microscopic creatures that can cause disease

Digestion

Like all animals, molluscs need to get **nutrients** into their bodies. This gives their organs and muscles a regular supply of energy. Plants contain many important nutrients that molluscs need to absorb in their stomachs. Juices and **acids** in their stomachs break down the food so that it can get into the blood. Waste material that cannot be digested goes into the **intestine** and is then passed out through the **anus**. This waste can often be found on lettuces or cabbages.

A slug's **radula** can have as many as 27,000 teeth. They rasp and rub rather than cut and chew like our teeth. Just like sharks, slugs lose and replace their teeth throughout their lives.

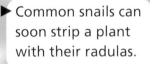

► Common snails can soon strip a plant with their radulas.

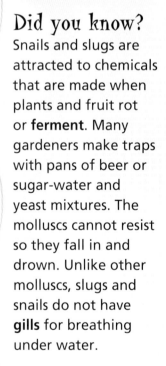

Did you know?

Snails and slugs are attracted to chemicals that are made when plants and fruit rot or **ferment**. Many gardeners make traps with pans of beer or sugar-water and yeast mixtures. The molluscs cannot resist so they fall in and drown. Unlike other molluscs, slugs and snails do not have **gills** for breathing under water.

---

intestine   part of the digestive system after the stomach
sediment   small particles that settle to the bottom of water

Predators

Many molluscs feed on smaller animals such as other tiny molluscs, **crustaceans**, fish or fish eggs. Some wait for these to drift by before they suck them in, while others go out hunting.

All **cephalopods** are **carnivores**. Like most other molluscs they have a **radula**, but they also have a pair of powerful, beak-like jaws. These jaws are strong and sharp so the animal can bite and tear apart its food.

Squid often dart up to a fish, grab it with their **tentacles** and bite a chunk out of its neck. Their tentacles are excellent for catching fish because they are covered in little suction cups. These suckers grip tightly to any surface. Large squid can be difficult to pull off an object they want to cling to.

Underwater vampire

One sea snail has been called the vampire snail as it feeds on the blood of sleeping parrot fish. It sneaks up on the parrot fish and clings on. It then bites round the fish's mouth and eats its blood.

▲ Here a sea snail is eating coral.

crustacean   sea animal with legs and a hard shell like crabs, lobsters and shrimp
host   animal that has a parasite living in or on its body

Parasites

A number of molluscs are **parasites**. This means they feed on other living animals. Many molluscs such as sea snails feed on sponges. The **host** sponge is not killed or eaten up completely, but it is damaged. Some sea snails also attach themselves to **coral**, starfish and sea urchins, and eat them.

The **larvae** of freshwater mussels are in danger of being swept away by the flowing water. They could easily be carried out to sea. To solve this problem, larvae of almost all freshwater mussels cling to the gills of fish and **survive** by being parasites. When they are big enough, the young mussels are able to let go of their free ride and can then live on their own on the riverbed.

▼ The beak of a giant squid can do some real damage to other sea animals.

Swapping roles

Mussel larvae use fish as hosts – but some fish use mussels as hosts! The bitterling (shown above) is a small fish that lays its eggs inside the common pond mussel's shell. The tiny bitterlings hatch and grow inside the mussel then swim away after a few weeks.

>>>>>>>>>
Find out more about parasite mussel larvae on page 31.

larvae   young of an animal that is very different from the adult
parasite   animal or plant that lives in or on another living thing

Breeding

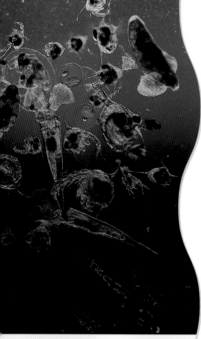

Molluscs have all sorts of ways of making new molluscs. But first they have to meet up.

Meeting and mating

Molluscs are silent so they rely on sight and scent to find a mate. Land snails and slugs follow slime trails to find each other. **Cephalopods** show off with dancing displays that attract partners. For many octopuses this is a dance of life and death, as shortly after mating they will die.

Cuttlefish also show off as they gather in large numbers. Rival males wave their **tentacles** at each other and their skin turns bright colours. Then they circle one another and copy each other's moves. The largest and most colourful male wins the female. He keeps waving his tentacles and flashing colours to impress his new partner.

New life

Mollusc eggs are part of the **plankton** floating in the sea. Most molluscs hatch from eggs as tiny **larvae**. They soon settle on the bottom of the sea or river. Here they mature and grow, if they can escape all the predators. Their shells soon form and protect them from hungry mouths. The plankton above are highly magnified.

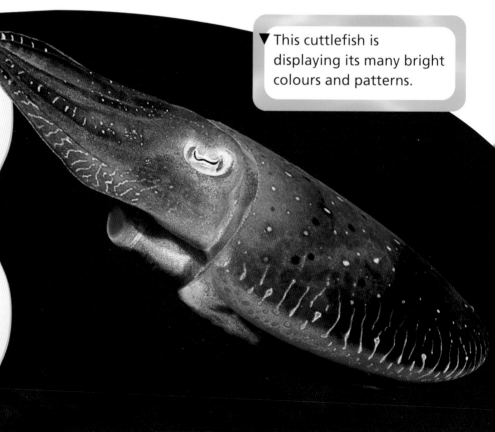

▼ This cuttlefish is displaying its many bright colours and patterns.

fertilize   when a sperm joins an egg to form a new individual
oviduct   tube in females that the eggs move through

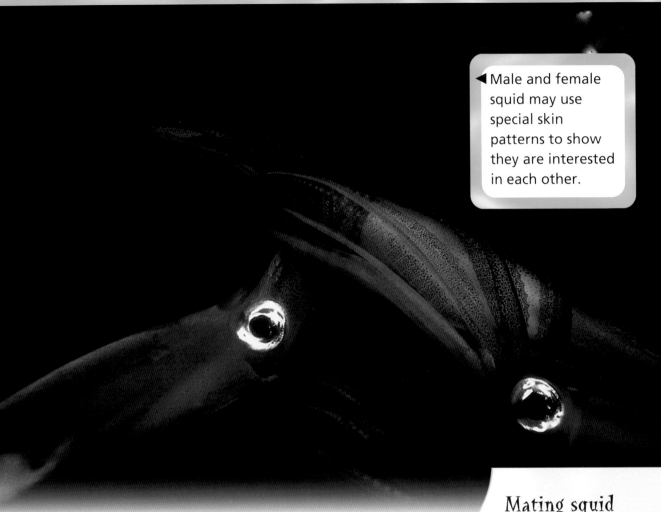

Male and female squid may use special skin patterns to show they are interested in each other.

Mating cuttlefish

Cuttlefish lock their tentacles together and **mate** facing each other. The male places a sealed **sperm** packet into a pouch just below the female's mouth. The female then hides in a den, which is usually a deep crack in the rocks. When she is safely inside, she draws each egg out of her body and passes it over the sperm. She lays up to 200 sticky white eggs.

The newly **fertilized** eggs hang from the rock in clusters. Tiny cuttlefish hatch out after four months. The young cuttlefish are just over 2 centimetres long and many are likely to be eaten by **predators**. Very few of the newly hatched cuttlefish **survive** their first few hours. Those that do survive grow quickly and move to deeper water.

Mating squid

The male squid takes a packet of sperm with one of his tentacles and plants it in the female's **oviduct**. Females then lay eggs, which stick to seaweed or to the sea-bed. The eggs of deep-water squid are left to drift around in the dark water. Many of them are eaten by fish.

sperm   male sex cell

Oyster eggs

Female oysters are champion egg-layers. Some may release over 1 million eggs in a season. Very few of these eggs will **survive** to become adult oysters. The manta ray below is feeding on **plankton** that includes oyster eggs in it.

Mating octopuses

When a male octopus is ready to mate, he moves close enough to the female to stretch out a **tentacle** and stroke her. His tentacle has a deep groove between the suckers. At the very end of the tentacle there is a spoon-like tip. He puts this under the female's **mantle**, and 'spoons' the **sperm** into the female's **oviduct**. She then swims off to find a safe den where she can lay her eggs. Sometimes, the male's arm can break off during mating and it gets stuck inside the female for a while. If this happens, the male simply grows a new one.

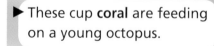

▶ These cup **coral** are feeding on a young octopus.

    mantle   fold of skin that covers the body

Eggs

A female octopus can lay 150,000 eggs over two weeks. She attaches them like a bunch of grapes to the roof of her rocky den. She will guard them for the next 50 days. To keep them clean and supplied with **oxygen**, she jets them with water. Then, when they are ready to hatch, she helps the young to escape from their eggs. Not long after her eggs hatch the female dies. Males die at about the same age as females.

The tiny young octopuses float up to the surface to feed. The few that avoid being eaten soon sink and quickly mature as they begin their life on the sea bed.

Egg champion

The giant clam like the one below can lay 1000 million eggs in one go. It may do this amazing act every year for 40 years or more. Just a few are ever likely to hatch. The rest become part of the mixture of tiny particles and plankton that many sea animals eat. Some giant clams may live for over 100 years.

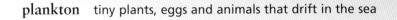

plankton   tiny plants, eggs and animals that drift in the sea

Born in the gills

Some female **bivalves**, such as the ones of the common oyster below, draw in water through their bodies. When this water has sperm in it, fertilization takes place inside the female's shell. The fertilized eggs then develop in the mother's gills.

Larvae

The European oyster and the Olympia oyster do not have to worry about meeting and mating. That is because they do it all themselves. Each oyster has both eggs and **sperm**. The eggs are **fertilized** inside the oyster's body and are kept in the **gills** until tiny **larvae** with soft shells are formed.

Bluepoint oysters have separate sexes. Females release millions of eggs into the water, where the males leave their sperm. The larvae develop within six hours and then swim about for two or three weeks. After that they settle among the stones, shells and gravel and begin to grow.

Some oysters care for their young inside their own shells until the tiny oysters are released on to the sea-bed.

bivalve   mollusc with two shells joined at a hinge
fertilize   when a sperm joins an egg to form a new individual

Hitching a ride

Tiny freshwater mussel larvae hatch and develop in their mother's gills for a while. But then it is time for a babysitter to take over. When a river trout swims by, the mussel lets her larvae go. The tiny mussels float up to the fish and cling on. They have little hooks to latch on to their new **host**.

The larvae live in their host's gills where they can filter the water flowing through for **oxygen** and **nutrients**. They also feed off the fish's body fluids. A tiny sac grows around them to keep them safe for what could be a few months. The foster parent does not have much choice but the larvae do not seem to harm it, unless lots of tiny mussels clog up its gills.

Life and death

Young cuttlefish are able to breed by the time they are two years old. After laying their eggs (shown above), the females lose strength and their bodies quickly close down. Their lives soon end and they never see their own young.

◀ A brown trout can be host to many mussel larvae.

---

gills flaps that some animals have to breathe under water
host animal or plant that has a parasite living in or on it

Defence

Eat me if you dare

Bright colours can be a warning to predators to keep off. Some molluscs have a painful sting, and looking scary can save them from being attacked. Others decorate themselves with other shells, pebbles or pieces of coral or weed so they cannot be seen.

The chance of a young mollusc making it to old age is slim. All molluscs have soft juicy bodies without bones. It is as though they are asking to be eaten. But they are not all easy targets. Many try to defend themselves.

Colour and camouflage

Predators are always on the look-out for a soft snack. But if no one can see you, you are likely to **survive** longer. So the trick is to disappear.

Many **cephalopods** are masters of **disguise**. They can change their colour and shape to blend in with their surroundings. Not only that, they can make patterns to help their **camouflage**. Some cephalopods flash four or five different patterns. This is enough to confuse or even **hypnotize** a predator for a few seconds – while the mollusc makes a quick getaway.

▲ A king scallop buries itself in the sand.

camouflage   colour that matches the background
disguise   change of appearance to look different

Extra powers

A cuttlefish can change colour in an instant. Even if it is put on top of different designs such as straight lines, zig-zags or check patterns, it is able to copy them exactly.

Some cuttlefish and many squid can glow in different colours. It is thought that about 80 per cent of all **species** living in the deep sea can make a special energy in their body cells that makes them glow with their own light. This serves two purposes. The light is a form of camouflage that breaks up the shape of their outline. This makes it difficult for a predator below to see the mollusc's shape against the surface light. The light may also attract mates.

Loud colours

Some sea slugs are brightly coloured to put predators off. A good example is this Spanish dancer, which only displays the brilliant red and white pattern on the side of its **mantle** when it is disturbed. In its silent world, it is a way of saying, 'Boo!'

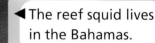

◄ The reef squid lives in the Bahamas.

Poison molluscs

Some of the smallest animals can pack the biggest punches. Two types of blue-ringed octopus are among the world's deadliest sea animals. They may look good to eat but they can kill you. They are found in rock pools around the coast of Australia. Although they are never bigger than 20 centimetres from the tip of one **tentacle** to another, they can kill quickly. The poison found in their **saliva** is so strong that just one of these octopuses could kill 26 humans in minutes.

Blue-ringed octopuses do not usually bother humans unless we pick them up or tease them. They normally look brown or yellow, but their blue rings appear when they are about to attack.

Pretty poison

Some tropical sea slugs warn **predators** that they are bad to eat. They come in many bright colours to warn they are filled with poison. If they are red with yellow **gills**, like the one below, they say to any enemy, 'Bite me if you dare... but it is the last thing you will do.'

antidote   medicine to make a poison safe
paralyse   stun an animal so that it is unable to move

Deadly

If a blue-ringed octopus strikes, it is hard to tell at first. You cannot tell you have been bitten immediately as there is no pain. But after just a few minutes you will feel sick and dizzy. Then the poison affects your senses and you lose your sight and sense of touch. Within a few more minutes the poison will **paralyse** you and it will be hard to breathe and swallow.

The only treatment is to get medical help fast, to keep your heart and lungs working. The poison has to work its way out of your system. There is no **antidote**. People have only **survived** when they have had quick medical help. So it is best not to mess with this deadly mollusc – which can even bite through a wetsuit.

Deadly shells

They look harmless but cone shells like the one above have tiny teeth like darts. They fire these at their **prey**. The darts inject strong **venom** that can even kill humans.

◄ The blue-ringed octopus can kill a human within an hour.

---

saliva   juices made in the mouth to help chewing and digestion
venom   poison

Armour

Most molluscs that surround themselves in tough shells have an excellent defence. Sea snails like the one above can quickly retreat into their armour-plated homes. Spikes and teeth at the shell mouth can stop predators getting inside. Some sea snails can also produce an ink cloud when in danger. People have used this ink as a purple dye.

Special tricks

One of the best defence tricks is to make a smoke screen to hide behind. Under water, it has to be an ink screen. Many **cephalopods** are able to squirt black ink to confuse enemies. Jets of ink cloud the water and allow a cephalopod to change direction as well as colour. Then it can escape while the inky water blocks the **predator's** view. Larger cephalopods do not tend to use ink as much as smaller ones.

The ink comes from a special sac that starts to work as soon as a young cephalopod hatches. However, those that live far down in the deep ocean do not have ink sacs, as they would be useless where the water is so dark.

▶ A giant octopus squirts a cloud of ink to keep a diver away.

mimic   someone who acts and pretends to be someone else

▼ This octopus is making itself look like a fierce lionfish.

A clever actor

One type of octopus is a skilful copycat. It is called a **mimic** octopus and it lives near the mouths of rivers in Indonesia. It was only discovered in 1998 when scientists saw it 'acting'. This octopus can turn into the shape of other animals to make its predators think that it is deadly. It can swim by waving its body just like a flatfish. This is probably to mimic soles, which have poisonous **glands**. It also pretends to be a lionfish or may try to look like the poisonous banded sea snake. To do this, the octopus buries six of its 60-centimetre long tentacles in the sand. Then it points just two **tentacles** in opposite directions and waves them, just like the movements of a snake.

Can you believe it?

The mimic octopus has been seen trying to behave like sand anemones and large jellyfish. Predators will not touch these creatures because of their **venom**. You cannot blame the octopus for trying to look scary.

Weird and wonderful

Disappearing giant

Giant clams are now an **endangered** species. They have been harvested for their meat, shells and to supply the aquarium trade, as they look stunning in tanks. Clam farms in Fiji are now trying to build up stocks of these rare molluscs.

Some of the bigger molluscs are incredible animals. For years these giants have amazed us.

Giant octopuses

The giant octopus is the largest **species** of octopus in the world. Although it is very unusual to find one over 45 kilograms, now and again some huge ones appear. In 1967, one was caught near Victoria in British Columbia, Canada. It weighed 70 kilograms and was 7.5 metres from one **tentacle** tip to another. Another was caught off the coast of New Zealand in 2002 and weighed 75 kilograms. There are other records of giant octopuses that weighed as much as 182 kilograms.

From time to time strange mounds of rubbery flesh are washed up on beaches. Some people think these could be the remains of massive octopuses.

endangered   at risk of disappearing forever

Massive molluscs

Although there have been a few reports of giant octopuses attacking humans, nothing has yet been proved. Nor have stories of man-eating clams. The giant clam has always been of interest to deep-sea divers. The largest known **bivalve** mollusc was a giant clam that weighed an amazing 333 kilograms. It was 1.4 metres wide.

This mollusc often gapes open like a large mouth waiting for small sea animals to swim inside. Then it closes and slowly digests its food. But a giant clam could only trap deep-sea divers if they were very slow. Clamping someone's feet would take a while as clams close quite slowly.

The shells of this mollusc have been used as children's bath tubs, and for **fonts** in many churches.

The biggest bivalve

Giant clams are found in the shallow waters of the Pacific Ocean, from Thailand and Japan to Australia. Adult giant clams are unable to move from their position on the coral reef. They stay in one place all their lives and suck in **plankton** to feed on.

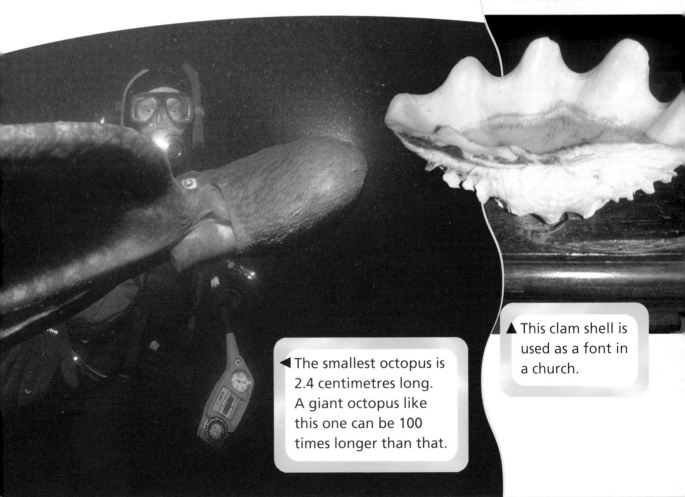

◄ The smallest octopus is 2.4 centimetres long. A giant octopus like this one can be 100 times longer than that.

▲ This clam shell is used as a font in a church.

font   basin to hold water to baptise babies in

▲ A sperm whale may be no match against a giant squid.

Giant squid

Far below the surface of the ocean lives a huge mollusc that few people have seen alive. Scientists travel down to the darkest depths of the ocean hoping to glimpse one of the most mysterious animals on earth – the giant squid.

Now and again this largest **invertebrate** of all time gets tangled in fishing gear and is dragged to shore. No giant squid has ever **survived** being caught. But they are out there in the deepest sea and some are enormous.

The largest of these squid was washed ashore on a New Zealand beach near Wellington in 1887. Its tentacles were 18 metres long and its body was over 2 metres long.

Fight to the death

In October 1966, two lighthouse keepers at Danger Point, South Africa, watched a baby sperm whale being attacked by a giant squid. 'The whale could only stay down for 10 minutes, then had to come up for air. It just had time to spout for a few seconds before being pulled down again.'

The squid finally won the contest and the baby whale was never seen again.

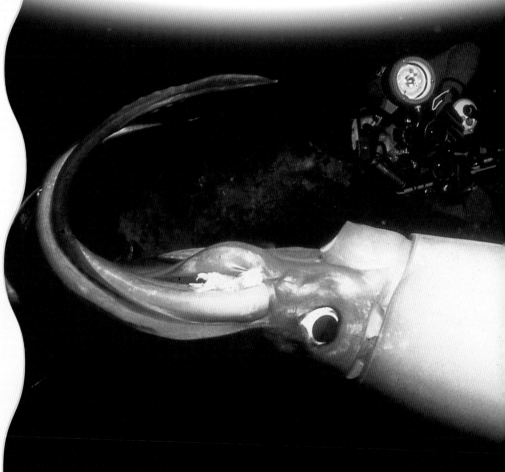

legend   old story based on some truth

Squid stories

Giant squid have sharp beaks that have been found in the stomachs of sperm whales. Sailors have sometimes seen whales and squid in fierce battles. It is thought that a giant squid can kill a huge whale. Whales have been found covered in marks from a squid's suckers.

Humans do not often meet up with giant squid. At least one report from World War II tells of survivors from a sunken ship being attacked by a giant squid that ate one of them.

Scientists have demonstrated that the blood of a giant squid does not carry **oxygen** very well in warm water. A squid might **suffocate** in warm water near the ocean surface. If so, it is hardly surprising they are so rarely seen.

True or false?

Maybe even larger squid lurk far below the ocean. Stories of huge squid have been the subject of **legends** for years. The famous sea monster called Kraken, reported in age-old tales, may well have links to giant squid. This huge beast was said to wrap its arms around ships and sink them.

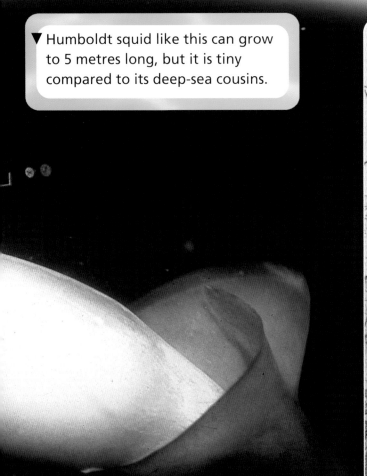

▼ Humboldt squid like this can grow to 5 metres long, but it is tiny compared to its deep-sea cousins.

suffocate   choke or die from being unable to breathe

How to make a pearl

An oyster makes a smooth substance called **nacre** to coat anything that gets into its shell. Nacre is made of minerals and proteins and it is the same material that coats the inside of its shell. It helps to keep its world silky smooth. It also makes pearls.

Giant pearls

Most molluscs with shells that live in water are able to make pearls. When grit or other material gets into their shell, they coat it with a substance similar to their shell lining to make it smooth. Some molluscs can grow pearls as big as golf balls.

It takes an oyster about two years to grow a pearl big enough to be used as jewellery. The older and bigger the pearl, the more valuable it is. Pearls from molluscs that do not normally produce them are particularly valuable. A large pearl from a pink conch sold for over US $4000 in 1999.

Pearls come in many colours including white, pink, silver, cream, gold and black. Pearls with pinkish-white or pinkish-silver colours have always been the most highly prized.

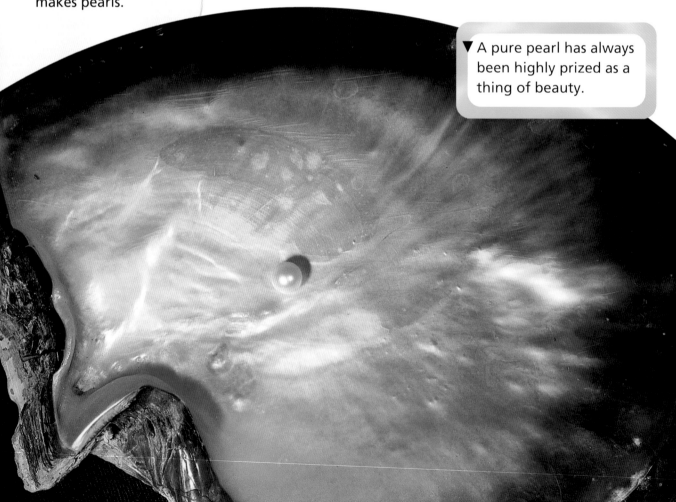

▼ A pure pearl has always been highly prized as a thing of beauty.

nacre   mother of pearl, a substance made by molluscs to coat the inside of their shells

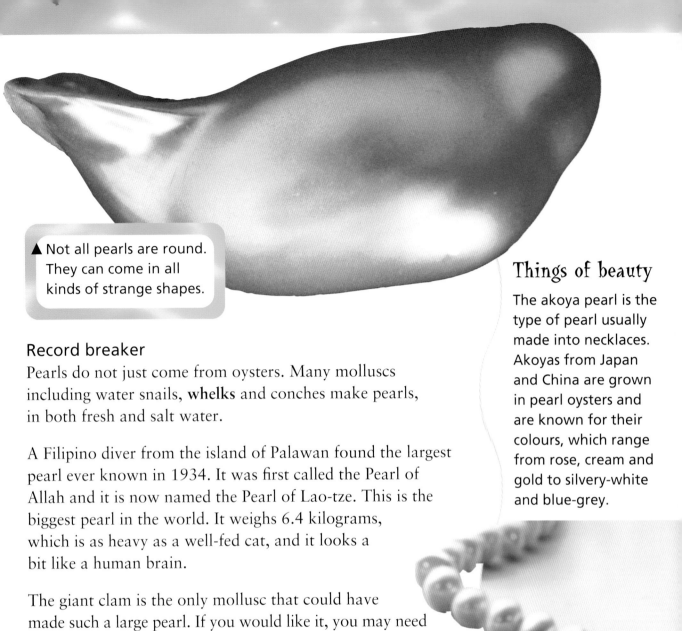

> ▲ Not all pearls are round. They can come in all kinds of strange shapes.

Things of beauty

The akoya pearl is the type of pearl usually made into necklaces. Akoyas from Japan and China are grown in pearl oysters and are known for their colours, which range from rose, cream and gold to silvery-white and blue-grey.

Record breaker

Pearls do not just come from oysters. Many molluscs including water snails, **whelks** and conches make pearls, in both fresh and salt water.

A Filipino diver from the island of Palawan found the largest pearl ever known in 1934. It was first called the Pearl of Allah and it is now named the Pearl of Lao-tze. This is the biggest pearl in the world. It weighs 6.4 kilograms, which is as heavy as a well-fed cat, and it looks a bit like a human brain.

The giant clam is the only mollusc that could have made such a large pearl. If you would like it, you may need to save up. It is estimated to be worth over US $40 million and it is kept in a San Francisco bank.

whelk   gastropod that lives in the sea and has a spiral shell

Giant snail

Scientists think the giant African snail is one of the most damaging land snails in the world. It comes from East Africa but it is now found in Asia, Hawaii and some appeared in Australia. It can eat through crops really fast.

You cannot blame the giant African snail. It was quite happy munching grass in Africa until people thought it would make a nice pet. So the giant snail began to appear in other countries and take over.

A boy returned to Miami from Hawaii in 1966 with three pet giant African snails. He let them go and seven years later more than 18,000 snails were found, along with masses of eggs. It took the State of Florida ten years and a lot of money to get rid of this pest.

Largest sea snails (length in centimetres)

Australian trumpet	80
horse conch	58
baler shell (above)	48
Triton trumpet	48

   hibernate 'close down' the body and rest when it is too cold or dry

Threat

So far, the USA and Australia have kept the giant snail under control. But if it gets a hold again, millions of dollars of food could be at risk.

This snail is tough. It can **survive** the cold – even snow. It simply slows down and **hibernates** until warm weather returns. So it could survive almost anywhere across the USA. It also breeds in bulk. After a single mating, both males and females lay a batch of 100–400 eggs. They can do this several times without mating again. In one year, each adult lays about 1200 eggs. Giant African snails can live as long as nine years, and that is enough time to make thousands of new snails. No wonder farmers must keep on the look-out for them.

Would you believe it?

The giant African snail is known to eat at least 500 different types of plants. Crops of cocoa, peanuts, rubber, beans, peas, cucumbers and melons can soon be destroyed by a few of these hungry molluscs. The poster below is to make people aware of the damage these snails can cause.

▼ A giant land snail in a farming area is Public Enemy Number 1.

Not All Alien Invaders Are From Outer Space

---

survive   stay alive despite difficulties and dangers

The wonderful world of slime

It is very useful to be able to ooze masses of slime whenever you want. You can slip away from anyone's grip. You can easily slide through narrow gaps. Slime is good for escaping and moving.

Slugs use slime for suction power when they travel upside down. They can then climb up trees, walls and even windows. Slugs leave a slime trail behind them as they move. This can be useful to let other slugs know where they are. But it can tell **predators** where they are, too.

Slime has a bad name, but it is useful stuff. It is a protective layer that keeps out nasty things – apart from salt. Salt is the one substance that a slug's slime cannot cope with. It makes a slug shrivel up and die.

Slimy friends

Banana slugs like the one above meet and **mate** in a thick goo of slime. Their slime must be delicious – as they often eat each other's slime before mating. How romantic!

▶ Slug pellets leave behind a shrivelled slug and plenty of slime.

drought   time with no rain and a shortage of water

Squelchy

When in danger, a slug is able to ooze a thick **mucus** coating and make its body shorter and fatter. This makes the slug more difficult to eat. The mucus also coats the slug in an unpleasant taste. Slugs can fit into almost any space when they become squelchy – long and thin or short and fat. Their slime helps them fit through tight squeezes. They can then avoid sunlight and heat by crawling into small damp crevices and holes.

Slime also stops a slug's body from drying out. This helps slugs **survive** during times of **drought**. Slugs have been seen eating their own slime trails. It is possible that slime could be healthy to eat – but only if you are a slug!

Slimy and safe

Snails' slime comes out from the front of their bodies and hardens when it comes into contact with air. The snail is able to move on very sharp pointed needles, over knife blades, razors, rocks and thorns without getting hurt because the mucus protects its body.

mucus   gummy, wet and slimy substance made by some plants and animals

Endangered

For all kinds of reasons, many animals are in danger of dying out. Some molluscs are among them. People may sometimes wonder if this matters. What do you think?

Saving snails

Three Australian land snails are listed as **endangered**. Since 1997, laws have been made to protect their **habitats** with the hope of preventing them from becoming **extinct**. One of these snails is found only in western Sydney in the Cumberland Plain Woodland. It is called *Meridolum*.

On the brink

The dwarf wedge mussel is a small, yellowish-brown freshwater mussel. It spends most of its time buried in the bottom of streams and rivers. This mussel was once found in fifteen rivers in eastern parts of North America. Its numbers have now dropped and very few are left. Water **pollution** caused by chemicals used in farming and projects such as the building of golf courses are blamed for the mussel's decline.

So will it make any difference if these molluscs disappear forever? When such **species** disappear, the whole **food chain** can be affected and other animals may die out or become endangered. We should protect our planet's animals for the future.

▼ This woodland habitat in Australia is protected to ensure that snails there do not become extinct.

extinct   died out, never to return
exotic   from strange and unusual foreign places

Queen conch

The queen conch was once found from the coasts of the Caribbean and the Bahamas to Florida and Bermuda. This **gastropod** can grow to 30 centimetres long and it moves by 'hopping', using its strong, **muscular** foot to throw itself forward. It may take up to 36 hours for these molluscs to produce between 300,000 and 750,000 eggs. Today there are very few queen conches left. This species has been overfished for food and for its attractive shell. Such conches were once used as a form of **currency** and were highly prized. They have recently been collected for tourists as they make **exotic** gifts and decorations for fish tanks and gardens.

Few left

One of the rarest snails in the UK is the sandbowl snail, shown below. It is very small, less than 1 centimetre long. It lives in damp hollows in sand dunes at just a few sites. Its numbers may have fallen because people have destroyed its habitat to develop golf courses or buildings.

▲ This queen conch shell has been made into an ornament.

food chain   order in which one living thing feeds on another
pollution   spoiling natural things by dangerous chemicals, fumes or rubbish

49

Medical molluscs

The deadly **venom** of some cone shells is today being used to help victims of **strokes** and heart disease. Scientists may soon produce a new drug from this to help control **chronic** pain.

FAST FACTS

- Snails have been a source of food and protein since Roman times.
- The French eat 40,000 tonnes of snails each year.

Molluscs and us

Molluscs matter. They are important to the whole balance of life on our planet. They give us food but they have other uses.

Over 1000 **species** of mollusc have been found deeper than 1.6 kilometres (1 mile) below the surface of the ocean. New species have been discovered since submarines have started to explore the ocean's deepest trenches. We still have much to find out about molluscs. Some may hold answers to all kinds of medical research.

Molluscs are already used in medicine. Ground oyster shells are used as **calcium** to help humans and animals develop strong bones and teeth. Oyster juice has been found to have chemicals that may help fight **viruses**. It might soon be made into useful drugs.

▶ The *Deep Star* research submarine can explore oceans over a kilometre deep.

chronic   very severe and long-lasting
stroke   illness caused when the flow of blood to the brain is interrupted

Danger

Molluscs can also bring misery. Snail fever causes great human suffering. This disease is also called bilharzia and affects 200 million people in Asia, the Pacific islands, Africa, the West Indies and South America. It is caused by the tiny **larvae** of a worm called a schistosome ('shis-ta-soam') that live in water snails. The snails are harmless but they let these worms **thrive**.

The tiny worms infect humans who wash or paddle in rivers. Within seconds, the **parasites** get through the skin and into the blood. They grow inside blood vessels and the lungs. If they get to the **intestines** or bladder, a victim grows very weak and can die. Destroying the snails is one way of stopping the deadly worms. Drugs can now kill them inside the body.

Mussel power

The threads that some mussels use to attach themselves to rocks are being tested as a possible glue in surgery. These threads are called 'byssal' which means 'fine linen'. Perhaps one day mussels may be used to repair muscles!

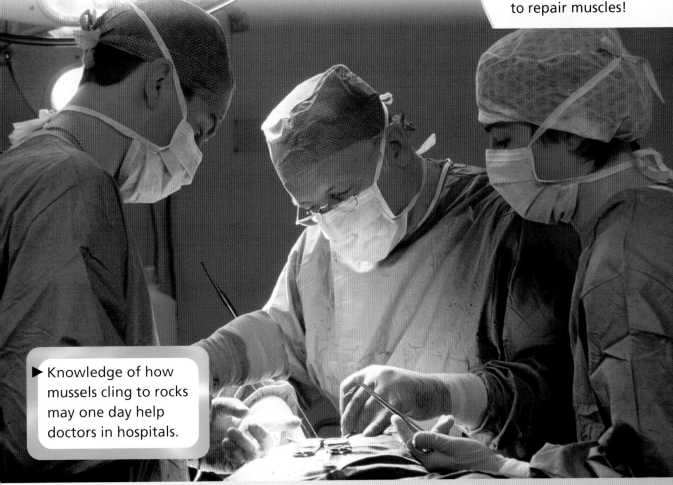

▶ Knowledge of how mussels cling to rocks may one day help doctors in hospitals.

---

thrive grow with strength and live healthily
virus organism that causes disease – only seen under a microscope

Find out more

Websites

Wonders of the sea: molluscs

Website with photos and information about molluscs.
oceanicresearch.org/ mollusk.html

The cephalopod page

Website with photos and information about octopuses, squid and cuttlefish.
dal.ca/~ceph/TCP/ index.html

The Learning Zone

Website with pictures, information and quizzes on molluscs.
www.oum.ox.ac/ children/fossils/ molluscs.html

Books

Gentle Giant Octopus (Read and Wonder), Karen Wallace (Walker, 2002)

Minibeasts: Slugs and Snails, Claire Llewellyn (Franklin Watts, 2002)

Variety of Life: Molluscs, Joy Richardson (Franklin Watts, 2003)

World Wide Web

If you want to find out more about molluscs, you can search the Internet using keywords like these:

- 'giant African snail'
- pearl + diving
- blue-ringed octopus

You can also find your own keywords by using headings or words from this book. Use the following search tips to help you find the most useful websites.

Search tips

There are billions of pages on the Internet so it can be difficult to find exactly what you are looking for.

For example, if you just type in 'water' on a search engine like Google, you will get a list of 50 million web pages! These search skills will help you find useful websites more quickly:

- Use simple keywords instead of whole sentences
- Use two to six keywords in a search, putting the most important words first
- Be precise – only use names of people, places or things
- If you want to find words that go together, put quote marks around them
- Use the advanced section of your search engine
- Use the + sign between keywords to link them. For example, typing + KS3 after your keyword will help you find web pages at the right level.

Where to search

Search engine

A search engine looks through a small proportion of the web and lists all sites that match the words in the search box. It can give thousands of links, but the best matches are at the top of the list, on the first page.
Try bbc.co.uk/search

Search directory

A search directory is like a library of websites that have been sorted by a person instead of a computer. You can search by keyword or subject and browse through the different sites like you look through books on a library shelf.
A good example is yahooligans.com

Numbers of incredible creatures

Bar chart showing number of species (approximate) for each creature group: Amphibians, Mammals, Reptiles, Birds, Fish, Arachnids, Molluscs, Insects. X-axis labelled "Number of species (approximate)" with scale 0, 20,000, 40,000, 60,000, 80,000, 100,000, 120,000, 140,000, 160,000, 180,000, 1,000,000. Y-axis labelled "Creatures".

Glossary

acid a liquid that can be strong enough to break down materials

adapt gradually change in a particular habitat

algae types of simple plant without stems that grows in water or on rocks

antidote medicine to make a poison safe

anus opening at the very end of the digestive passage

bacteria group of microscopic creatures that can cause disease

bivalve mollusc with two shells joined at a hinge

calcium mineral that animals need in food for strong bones and teeth

camouflage colour that matches the background

carnivore meat-eater

cephalopod ('sef-a-la-pod') mollusc that has tentacles coming from its head

chronic very severe and long-lasting

chiton ('ky-ton') a mollusc with an oval shell made up of eight overlapping plates.

cilia tiny hairs that wave together to make currents of movement

cockle sea mollusc that has a ribbed bivalve shell

complex detailed and complicated

coral tiny sea animals with hard outer casings that live together in large colonies

crustacean sea animal with jointed legs and a hard shell such as a crab or lobster

currency money of an area or good used for trading and exchange

current body of water that moves in a particular direction

disguise change of appearance to look different

drought time with no rain and a shortage of water

endangered at risk of disappearing forever

exotic from strange and unusual foreign places

extinct died out, never to return

ferment when sugar in food turns to alcohol

fertilize when a sperm joins an egg to form a new individual

font basin to hold water to baptise babies in

food chain order in which one living thing feeds on another

gastropod invertebrate that moves along on its soft belly

gills flaps that some animals have to breathe under water

gland part of the body that makes hormones and other substances

habitat natural home of an animal or plant

herbivore animal that only eats plants – a vegetarian

hibernate 'close down' the body and rest when it is too cold or dry

hinge movable joint, like the part that fixes a door to a frame but allows it to open and close

host animal or plant that has a parasite living in or on it

hypnotize send someone into a trance

intestine part of the digestive system after the stomach

invertebrate animal without a backbone

larva (plural: **larvae**) young of an animal that is very different from the adult

legend old story based on some truth

lens clear, curved part of the eye

mantle fold of skin that covers the body

mate when a male and female animal come together to produce young

mimic someone who acts and pretends to be someone else

mucus gummy, wet and slimy substance made by some plants and animals

muscular has strong muscles

nacre mother of pearl, a substance made by molluscs to coat the inside of their shells

native belonging to that particular place

nutrients important substances found in food and needed by the body

oviduct tube in females that the eggs move through

oxygen one of the gases in air and water that all living things need

paralyse stun an animal so that it is unable to move

parasite animal or plant that lives in or on another living thing

plankton tiny plants, eggs and animals that drift in the sea

pollution spoiling natural things by dangerous chemicals, fumes or rubbish

predator animal that hunts and eats other animals

prey animal that is killed and eaten by other animals

propel drive or push forward

radula long, rough tongue like a file

saliva juices made in the mouth to help chewing and digestion

scallop a bivalve mollusc with semicircular shells with wavy edges

sediment small particles that settle to the bottom of water

species type of animal or plant

sperm male sex cell

stroke illness caused when the flow of blood to the brain is interrupted

suffocate choke or die from being unable to breathe

survive stay alive despite difficulties and dangers

tentacle animal body part that is like a long, thin arm

thrive grow with strength and live healthily

venom poison

virus organism that causes disease – only seen under a microscope

whelk gastropod that lives in the sea and has a spiral shell

Index

Series in the *Freestyle Curriculum Strand* include:

Turbulent Planet

Energy Essentials

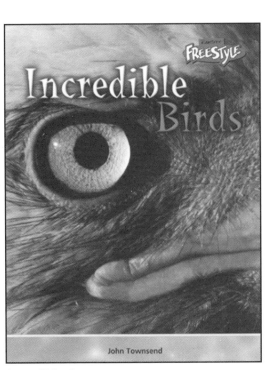

Incredible Creatures

Material Matters

Find out about the other titles in these series on our website www.raintreepublishers.co.uk